# TaeKwonDo – W

## Your Ultimate Grading and Reference Summary Guide

**Phil Pierce**



For a Free Martial Arts guide visit:
www.PhilPierceBooks.com

This guide is not associated with any Martial Arts organization. All content herein is considered a guide only.

No liability accepted for any injury associated with the practice of Martial Arts, Self Defense or any other activity.

# What Can You Get From This Book?

- **Do you know how to develop Speed and Strength essential for grading?**
- **The exact requirements for grading at each stage?**
- **White to Black Belt Training**
- **The essential Code of Conduct and Top Tips**
- **Set and Free Sparring requirements**
- **Belt Colors and their symbolism**
- **Patterns**

*Unlocking the often mysterious world of Martial Arts, this book gives you the essential inside information for grading at every stage in Taekwondo!*

Broken down into easy-to-use Belt categories and tips this guide is the perfect accompaniment to in-class training or for revision and grading preparation. Get the edge in your training today!

TAEKWONDO
태 권 도

# From the Author

**Hi, and a warm welcome to the Ultimate Grading Guide, giving you the inside information essential for every Tae Kwon Do student. Taking you all the way from White to Black Belt.**

Over the years I have been lucky enough to train around the world in a variety of styles but I will always have a special place for Taekwondo, as the first Martial Art I became involved with.

With that in mind, I created this book to help those involved with TKD better understand the training and requirements for advancing to the next level and improving their skills.

This guide is broken into each belt category to help you find exactly what you need for your next grading, and make it that little bit less nerve wracking when the day comes!.

Just look for the belt colors at the top of the pages to find the page you need. Not only do you have the specific information for your grade but the general information at the front serves as a reminder for some often forgotten principles of being a TaeKwonDo student and for practicing martial arts as a whole.

Of course nothing beats practice and this guide is best used as an addition to regular in-class sessions. Also remember that grading requirements vary massively around the world. Every club and instructor has their own ways of ensuring students make the grade. This guide covers many of the basics from the most common requirements around the world but check locally to see how things are done where you are.

Good Luck!

- ***Phil***

# Foreword: How to Use This Guide

**There are hundreds, if not thousands of variations in Taekwondo styles around the world. The information in this book contains techniques and guidelines for training mainly in TAGB, ITF and other European styles, based on my experiences and the most common techniques I have encountered.**

Some of the content however, may not identically match your local requirements. Check your own syllabus for details.

Many of the tips though, are universal for all students and can help you in better understanding how to improve your training and understanding of Taekwondo in any style.

**So where are the pictures of...?**

Although this guide includes some general imagery you may find it doesn't include images of every specific technique or pattern. This book is aimed as a handy supplement to physical in-class training, not a replacement for it.

Additionally by including hundreds of extra pages this guide would become a large tome full of a possibly overwhelming amount of information. Better to have a short summary and remember what you need, than learn everything and remember nothing!

Develop your techniques in class and use this revision guide to sharpen up your knowledge when you need to.

If you are interested in checking out detailed breakdowns of techniques there are numerous books and videos to enhance your learning and included at the end are further reads to improve your Martial Arts training in general.

# What's Your Style? (Embrace the differences)

**Like many Martial Arts Taekwondo has evolved all around the world into a huge number of slightly different styles and organizations.**

This diversity creates an exciting and dynamic community of enthusiasts which all offer different perspectives on, what is at least on paper, the same art. Do you train in ITF styles? (using hands and legs equally) or do you focus on a WTF method of training? (The Olympic style more focused on kicks).

Or perhaps you sit somewhere in between, with techniques pulled in from many different groups. Whatever your allegiance, it's important to A. Recognize there will be differences around the world and B. Accept these without negative judgment.

Often the difference between a skilled, knowledgeable Martial Artist and one that is simply in it for ego can be spotted in their attitude to other arts.

Similarly this book is aimed at a certain couple of styles, the most commonly practiced based on my experience; (TAGB, ITF and European styles). It would be nearly impossible to cover all the regional variations around the world and so the more popular and universal requirements have been included where possible.

Most of the techniques and syllabus included will follow these styles but I almost guarantee that there will be differences, especially if you practice an alternative method at your club.

But the essence of Taekwondo and the many guiding principles are universal, so even if you don't train in one of the above styles you will still find useful information and general guidance on being a good student.

Opening yourself to knowledge from all sources is important to succeed as a rounded Martial Artist.

# A History of Taekwondo

**As a martial art TaeKwonDo has evolved into a modern form of both sport and self-defense and, in terms of student numbers, is the most popular martial art practiced on the planet.**

The current forms of Tae Kwon Do practiced are an evolution of combined styles of martial arts and self-defense techniques from both Korea and its surrounding area, from the last 2000 years.

Indeed many draw comparisons between TaeKwonDo and the sharp linear forms of Japanese Karate (particularly Shotokan) and also some of the circular Chinese Kung Fu techniques.

Not surprisingly many eastern martial arts are also seen to be hybrids of other styles, at least in part. The feudal old days of the far-east led to many conflicts between warring nations and any effective techniques were soon adopted by an opposing force and passed down through the generations.

TaeKwonDo however, has its roots more closely linked to Taek-Kyon and Subak as early forms of the art, used by the Hwarang - a warrior group in Korea during the Silla dynasty.

In its current form TaeKwonDo was inaugurated at a conference on 11th April 1955 thanks largely to the efforts of influential figure General Hong Hi Choi combining elements of Taek-Kyon and Karate.

Today there are many more aspects to TaeKwonDo than just fending off invaders. In fact it is more than just a physical skill of fighting (although that is part of it). It represents a way of thinking and a way of living according to strict discipline and morals.

The theory is that we are not just training our bodies but also our minds to make the right choices within our daily lives and, should the need arise, we will be able to use our skills for the greater good.

Above all show respect, work hard and enjoy your training on the path to Black Belt and beyond!

*This is only a guide and all gradings are at examiners discretion.

# Introduction to 'TaeKwonDo'

**The unarmed defense system known as TaeKwonDo can be traced to the Orient where it has been practiced for centuries. This designates TaeKwonDo as ancient marital art form. The modern version which is practiced today was created in Korea.**

The Korean translation for the TaeKwonDo is broken down into three parts. First, the term "Tae" renders an action with the foot such as to jump, smash, or kick. Next, the middle portion "Kwon" converts to the term "fist" meaning, punches or destruction via the hand. Finally we come to "Do" which yields the "way", "method", or "art".

This translation aptly describes the TaeKwonDo unarmed combat system which is made up of intricate kicks and punches, dodges, blocks and interceptions. With proper execution, these techniques join to allow the practitioner to swiftly overpower an opponent.

For the Korean people the TaeKwonDo practice represents much more than a grouping of defense techniques. To them it also encompasses a lifestyle and philosophy. It is used to impart lessons in self-discipline and encourage a strong moral grounding.

TaeKwonDo may be used to combat the fears, pressures, and violence of modern life. Through the practice of this martial art form a previously weak individual can gain the strength and confidence to defend themselves against any threat. Still, it much be practiced with care as the power behind TaeKwonDo can prove lethal if misused.

# The Five Tenets of TaeKwonDo

**Although the specifics vary from place to place the most common guiding principles behind TaeKwonDo remain the same.**

*1. Ye-Ui - Courtesy*
*2. Yom-Chi - Integrity*
*3. In-Nae - Perseverance*
*4. Kuk-Chi - Self-Control*
*5. Baekju- Bool-Gool- Indomitable Spirit*

# Understanding the Five Tenets of TaeKwonDo

***Courtesy:*** A student must demonstrate respect for their teachers, comrades, and the TaeKwonDo traditions. Proper etiquette and manners are also expected at all times and in all locations.

***Integrity:*** This means that those who practice TaeKwonDo should abide by what is right and stand against what is wrong. They must possess a conscience and experience guilt when they fail to stay within the boundaries of what is right. They are expected to always stand up for what is right.

***Perseverance:*** In order to reach a goal an individual must carry on despite challenges, failures, or hardships until they reach the intended target no matter how long it may take.

***Self-control:*** A student must master control of their physical actions as well as their thoughts.

***Indomitable Spirit:*** This means that an individual is required to find the courage to stand by their beliefs in the face of adversity. They must apply all of their energy to everything that they do.

# The International TaeKwonDo Oath

**Many variations exist of the oath taken before gradings or practice of Taekwondo, however they all share the same themes;**

The International TaeKwonDo Oath focuses on: Observation of the Tenets of Tae Kwon-Do, Respect for Teachers and Seniors (and fellow students), Never Misusing your skills, becoming a proponent of Freedom and Justice and, overall, promoting world peace

# Understanding the International TaeKwonDo Oath

**Observation of the Tenets:**
A student is obliged to commit to the five tenets of TaeKwonDo. They must both acknowledge and consistently adhere to each of them.

**Respect for Teachers and Seniors (and fellow students**

The student pledges to show reverence towards their instructors, and individuals who are presented as their seniors whether by age or ranking. The instructors must also return that respect to all individuals including their students. Thus both parties gain respect by demonstrating their ability to respect others. Failing to uphold this portion of the pledge constitutes a misuse of TaeKwonDo

**Never Misusing your skills**

Any misuse of TaeKwonDo whether to achieve personal gains or hurt another individual is wrong and goes against the international oath.

**Becoming a proponent of Freedom and Justice**

This portion of the oath applies to all aspects of the student's life. Though this may seem like a large undertaking, this promise can be upheld through small but positive deeds. This may include opening ones minds to the beliefs of others so as to eliminate any pre-judgments. As a result your world will be transformed into a zone of acceptance and understanding. Giving individuals this freedom welcomes more justice into existence.

**Promoting world peace**

This last portion is achieved by living your own life with peace. Though simplistic, if we all lived in a peaceful manner the world would inherently become a place of peace. Living peacefully does not insinuate that defending against an attack is wrong. Still, it is important to know the difference between defending against an unavoidable threat and provoking violence which violates this oath.

# Top Tips

**The following tips are taken from Practise Guidelines from a variety of styles. Most focus on being a good student through diligence and perseverance.**

1. Be a motivated learner by maintaining a thirst for continued progress. Know that the capacity to learn new things exists at all times in all locations.

2. Be willing to make sacrifices for your TaeKwonDo practice and teacher. Simply paying your monthly dues will not increase your proficiency. Participating in demonstrations, lessons, and being an active member at your Dojang will prove more effective.

3. Set a positive example for beginning students. They will naturally try to model the higher-ranking practitioners whom they wish to become.

4. Remain loyal to the TaeKwonDo art and your teacher. Always treat them respectfully and never criticize their efforts.

5. Learn, practice, and make use of every technique you are taught.

6. Maintain proper conduct both inside and outside the Dojang. Your actions will reflect upon your own character as well as the honour of your teacher, and the art of TaeKwonDo.

7. Abandon any training from alternate Dojangs which is not approved by your teacher. If you refuse to do this you should return to the Dojang in which you learned those habits and continue your practice there.

8. Remain respectful towards your teacher. If a disagreement arises, continue to follow your instructor's directions and address the matter following the session.

9. Foster your training by paying close attention, asking questions and maintaining enthusiasm.

10. Remain trustworthy.

# Code of Conduct Inside the "Dojang"

**Correct behavior in your training hall is important. Not just to preserve the sanctity of Taekwondo but because developing discipline and good habits will improve your techniques when grading or under pressure.**

**Each TaeKwonDo student is expected to follow a respectful code of conduct within the Dojang. Within the walls of the training hall follow the expectations listed below.**

1. Always bow when you enter the gym and again before leaving.

2. Always bow to your teacher while maintaining the proper spacing.

3. Students should exchange greetings.

4. When a group of students forms a line to participate in a training exercise they must bow to their teacher before the instruction begins.

5. Always recite the international TaeKwonDo oath (even if only mentally) at the start of instruction.

6. Address every instructor or black belt respectfully and using the title "Sir" or "Miss".

# Why Patterns?

Even those from outside of Martial Arts are usually familiar with how patterns look.

**In TaeKwonDo patterns are groupings of basic movements which are used to create an effective defense or attack. These are arranged in a concrete and logical order. Most of the patterns allow a student to defend against multiple theoretical opponents while making use of various blocking and attacking techniques oriented in an array of directions.**

This practice permits a student to execute a series of the fundamental skills. The result is the development of sparring techniques, flexibility, muscle strength, breath control, rhythm, weight shifting, and fluidity. Patterns allow a student to gain techniques not directly accessible through the fundamental exercises or sparring practice.

If one were to consider each fundamental movement or training exercise as one letter in an alphabet, then each pattern becomes a single word within the language of TaeKwonDo. Patterns constitute a succession of sparring techniques, tests of power, and inspiring feats. Patterns are beautiful.

The ability to practice sparring with an opponent may demonstrate an individual's capabilities, but the real test of their technique is the proper execution of patterns.

## *Top tips when practicing patterns:*

1. Always start and end in the same spot (if required) to demonstrate your ability to perform each pattern accurately.

2. Maintain proper posture and stance throughout the pattern. Be aware of the direction you are facing at all times.

3. Be conscious of which moments your muscles should be tense and when to relax.

4. Perform each exercise with rhythm and be sure to exhibit a sense of ease as opposed to stiff, awkward movements.

5. Complete a pattern at the speeds presented by your teacher. Decelerate and accelerate when appropriate.

6. Master one pattern before attempting the next one.

7. Seek out and remember the purpose of each movement.

8. Complete every pattern with a sense of realism.

# The Secret to Speed and Strength

**If you've ever seen a pattern or floor work performed in any Martial Art you've no doubt spotted how obvious it becomes when a student is strong and sharp – creating a powerful looking sequence or conversely if a student is hesitant and lackluster with their techniques.**

The difference is night and day and if you are an instructor or involved with grading you will instantly be able to pick out those students you already know will pass and those you need to keep an eye on more closely.

So what is the secret to looking sharp within a grading environment?

**Beginning and Ending**

The easiest tip to remember is to start and finish strong in any given sequence, making sure your starting and finishing strike or stance is emphasized.

This is not to say you can slack off with the middle techniques but the very first and very last techniques are typically the ones that grading examiners will notice the most.

First because it is your opening impression to them and the start of the sequence, and last because you often have to hold this position longer than the others.

**Developing Power**

Power is what really makes the difference between a great student and a mediocre one. If you can demonstrate this you are already ahead of the curve.

But what is Power?

For our purposes Power can technically be defined as Speed x Strength but developing these individually will not suddenly give you the magic formula.

A certain type of exercise known as Plyometrics are generally regarded as the best for developing power, which is perfect for Martial Artists. (You can grab a free guide to Plyometric Power on my site at www.PhilPierceBooks.com)

Essentially we are aiming to develop 'snappiness'. A certain explosive power that shows both speed and strength but also precision and control.

If for example you throw a punch you would make it quick, (but not rushed) Strong, (but not over-tense) and then stop it quickly and accurately.

This demonstrates control over your abilities but also that if you connected with them they could do damage. We are, after all, simulating fighting techniques aimed at taking out an opponent.

**Think About the Application**

Which leads us nicely to the last point in making your techniques look good.

It's easy to forget that all the methods we use are basically ways of incapacitating an opponent. Sure, they may be fairly abstract by today's standards and it can be tricky to spot the application of some blocks or strikes, but in essence you should perform each maneuver as if your life depended on it!

If you throw a punch that would barely tickle your opponent's nose it's not only and insult to the art but looks terrible to anyone watching and will lose you serious points in a grading environment.

Always consider if the effort you are using could work in real life.

# Belt Requirements

**The following pages detail the specific requirements for grading, and in turn gaining your belt, at the various levels in TaeKwonDo. Practice in class is essential to perfecting the physical techniques but these summaries can be invaluable in revision before a grading or as a reminder to your formal sessions.**

As with most of this guide your local requirements may vary but even if your requirements are slightly different the Korean terminology, color symbolism and associations are useful to know for all students.

# White Belt (Ninth Kup)

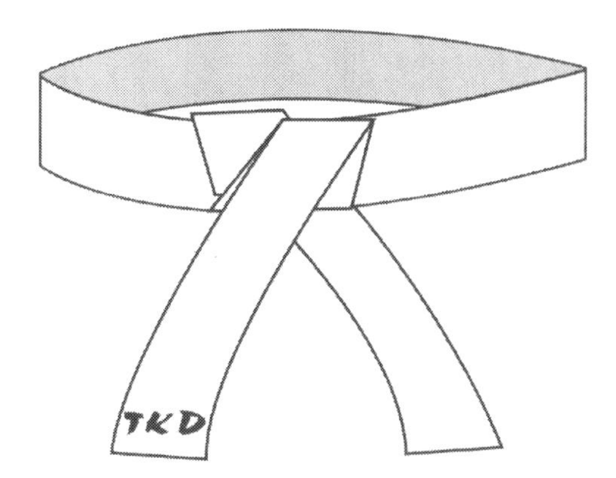


## *Requirements:*

1. Basic Sitting Stance with Single Punch
2. Front Facing Rising Kicks
3. Ten Press-ups
4. Four Direction Punching ( Sajo Jirugi)
5. Basic Walking Stance with Forward and Back Middle Section Punch
6. Basic Walking Stance with Forward and Back Low Block and Reverse Punch
7. Basic Walking Stance with Forward and Back Middle Block and Reverse Punch

## *White Belt Symbolism*

The white belt and color white symbolizes innocence. These students are just beginning their TaeKwonDo journey.

## *Terminology*

| **Korean** | **Number** |
|---|---|
| - Anna | One (1) |
| - Dol | Two (2) |
| - Set | Three (3) |

| | |
|---|---|
| - Net | Four (4) |
| - Dasul | Five (5) |
| - Yosul | Six (6) |
| - Ilgop | Seven (7) |
| - Yodull | Eight (8) |
| - Ahop | Nine (9) |
| - Yoll | Ten (10) |

| **Korean** | **Translation** |
|---|---|
| Dwiyro Torro | About Turn (Motion) |
| Cheryot | (Come to) Attention |
| Cheryot Sogi | Attention Stance |
| Dwiyro Kaggi | Backwards (Motion) |
| Ti | Belt |
| Kyong Ye | (After Cheryot) Bow |
| Haessan | To Dismiss (the Class) |
| Tae Kwon-Do | Foot-Fist-Art |
| Palmok | Forearm (Area) |
| Ap Joomuk | Forefist |
| Saju Jirugi | Four Directional Punching |
| Apro Kaggi | Forward (Motion) |
| Ap Chaolligi | Front Rising Kick |
| Nopunde | High Section |
| An-Palmok Makgi | Inner (Arm area) Forearm Block |
| An-Pamok | Inner Forearm (Arm Area) |
| Sabum | Instructor |
| Najunde | Low Section |
| Kaunde | Middle Section |
| Baro Jirugi | Obverse (forward) Punch |
| Bakat Palmok Makgi | Outer (Arm Area) Forearm Block |
| Bakat Palmok | Outer Forearm |
| Narani Sogi | Parallel Stance |
| Chunbi | Ready |
| Barro | Return to Ready Stance Position |
| Bandae Jirugi | Reverse Punch |
| Yop Chaolligi | Side Rising Kick |
| Annun Sogi | Sitting Stance |
| Si-Jak | Start |
| Gomman | Stop |
| Jeja | Student |

| | |
|---|---|
| Do-jang | Training Hall |
| Dobuk | Training Suit |
| Gunnun Sogi | Walking Stance |

# White Belt Pattern: Saju Jurugi (1&2)

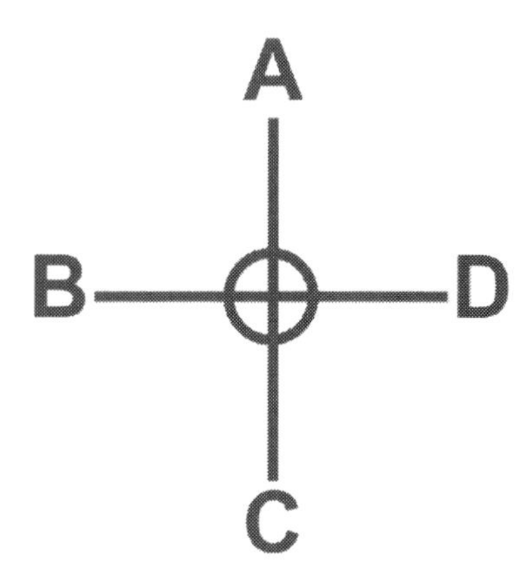


*Start:*

1. Bring the right foot in the direction of A, creating a right oriented walking style stance. Execute an obverse style middle section punch.

2. Step your right foot backward and towards the left. Next, move it back into a left side walking stance in the direction of B. Complete and obverse style low section outer oriented block with your forearm.

3. Shift your right foot in the direction of B, creating a right walking stance. Initiate an obverse middle section punch.

4. Return your right foot to the left. Bring the right foot backward, creating a left walking style stance oriented in the direction of C. Complete an obverse low section outside block with your forearm.

5. Bring your right foot to the front in the direction of C, creating a right walking stance. Execute an obverse middle section punch.

6. Return your right foot to the left. Step the right foot backward into a left side walking stance oriented in the direction of D. Complete an obverse style low section outer block with your forearm.

7. Shift your right foot in the direction of D, creating a right walking stance. Execute an obverse middle section punch.

8. Move your right foot backwards into a parallel ready stance oriented in the direction of A.

9. Shift your left foot in the direction of A, creating a left side walking stance. Complete an obverse middle section punch.

10. Return your left foot to the right. Next, shift the left foot backward to create a right walking stance oriented in the direction of D. Execute an obverse low section outer block with your forearm.

11. Shift your left foot in the direction of D, creating a left side walking stance. Complete an obverse middle section punch.

12. Return your left foot to the right. Next, shift the left backward to create a right walking stance oriented towards C. Execute an obverse low section outer block with your forearm.

13. Bring your left foot in the direction of C, creating a left side walking stance. Complete an obverse middle section punch.

14. Work your left foot back to the right. Next, shift it towards the back to create a right walking stance oriented in the direction of B. Execute an obverse low section outer block with your forearm.

15. Bring your left foot closer to B, creating a left side walking stance. Complete an obverse middle section punch.

* Perform Saju Jurugi (2) by following the same sequence but substitute each low section outer block with your forearm, with a middle section inner block with the forearm.

# Yellow Stripe Belt (Ninth Kup)

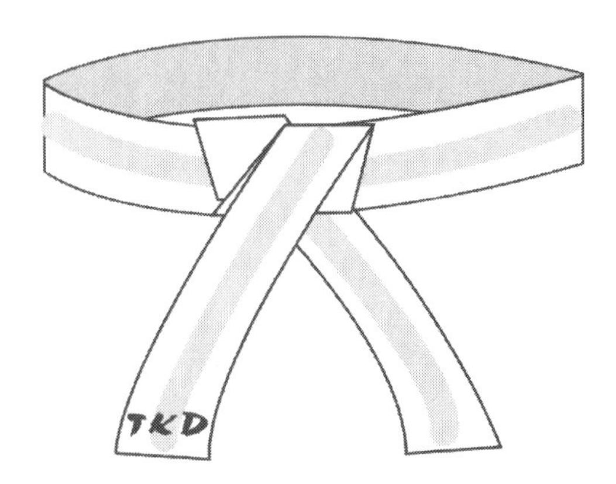


## *Requirements:*

1. Sitting Stance with Double Punch
2. Walking Ready Stance with Front Kick
3. Walking Stance with Double Punch
4. L-Stance with Middle Block
5. L-Stance with Knife-hand Strike
6. Walking Stance with Low Block and Rising Block
7. Pattern: Chon-ji

## *Yellow Belt Symbolism*

The colour yellow symbolizes the earth upon which seeds have been planted and are just beginning to sprout stems and roots. Here a solid bedrock of TaeKwonDo basics is being laid.

## *Terminology*

| **Korean** | **Translation** |
|---|---|
| Ap-Kumchi | Ball of the Foot |
| Balkal | Footsword (Part of foot in Sidekick) |
| Palmok | Forearm |
| Ap Chabusigi | Front Snap Kick |
| Daebi Makgi | Guarding Block |

| | |
|---|---|
| Mori | Head |
| Chagi | Kick |
| Niunja Sogi | L-Stance |
| Wen | Left |
| Tul | Pattern |
| Momtong-Bachia | Press Ups |
| Orun | Right |
| Chookyo Makgi | High Rising Block |
| Sambo Matsoki | Three-Step Sparring |

# Yellow Stripe Belt Pattern: Chon Ji

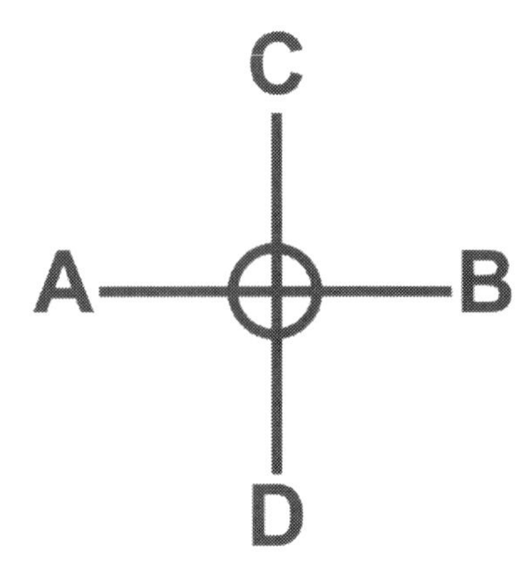


*The terms Chon and Ji can be translated to "the heaven" and "the earth" respectively. Within the Orient Chon Ji is accepted as either the creation of the world or beginning of our history. Thus it makes sense that this is one of the earliest patterns taught to TaeKwonDo beginners. It includes 19 movements which are broken down into two sections, the first signifies heaven, and the second signifies earth.*

***Start:*** Begin this pattern in a parallel ready stance. Stand along the AB line and face in the direction of D.

1. Bring your left foot towards B to create a left side walking stance oriented in the direction of B. Complete a left low section forearm block also in the direction of B.

2. Step your right foot towards B to create a right walking stance oriented in the direction of B. Complete a right middle section punch also in the direction of B.

3. Work your right foot towards A. Rotate towards the right, creating a right walking style stance oriented in the direction of A. Perform a right low section forearm block also in the direction of A.

4. Bring your left foot towards A, creating a left side walking stance in the direction of A. Complete a left middle section punch also in the direction of A.

5. Step the left foot towards D, creating a left side walking stance in the direction of D. Perform a left low section forearm block also in the direction of D.

6. Work your right foot towards D, creating a right walking stance in the direction of D. Complete a right middle section punch also in the direction of D.

7. Bring your right foot towards C. Rotate towards the right to create a right walking stance oriented in the direction of C. Perform a right low section forearm block also in the direction of C.

8. Step your left foot towards C, creating a left side walking stance oriented in the direction of C. Perform a left middle section punch also in the direction of C.

9. Work your left foot towards A, creating a right side L-Stance oriented in the direction of A. Complete a left inner oriented middle section forearm block also in the direction of A.

10. Bring your right foot towards A, creating a right walking stance oriented in the direction of A. Perform a right middle section punch also in the direction of A.

11. Step your right foot towards B. Rotate to the right, creating a left side L-Stance oriented in the direction of B. Complete a right middle section inner forearm block.

12. Work your left leg towards B, creating a left side walking stance oriented in the direction of B. Perform a left middle section punch also in the direction of B.

13. Bring your left foot towards C, creating a right L-stance oriented in the direction of C. Complete a left middle section forearm block also in the direction of C.

14. Step your right foot towards C, creating a right walking stance oriented in the direction of C. Perform a right middle section punch also in the direction of C.

15. Work your right foot towards D. Rotate towards the right, creating a left side L-Stance oriented in the direction of D. Complete a right middle section inner forearm block also in the direction of D.

16. Bring your left foot towards D, creating a left side walking stance oriented in the direction of D. Perform a left middle section punch also in the direction of D.

17. Step your right foot towards D, creating a right walking stance oriented in the direction of D. Complete a right middle section punch also in the direction of D.

18. Work your right foot towards C, creating a left side walking stance oriented in the direction of D. Perform a left middle section punch in the direction of D.

19. Bring your left foot towards C, creating a right walking stance oriented in the direction of D. Complete a right middle section punch in the direction of D.

* Finish the pattern by moving your left foot backwards, establishing the ready posture.

# Yellow Belt (Eighth Kup)

## *Requirements:*

1. L-Stance with Twin Forearm Block
2. Walking Stance with Front Kick and Double Punch
3. L-Stance with Inward Block
4. Turning Kick with Guarding Block
5. L-Stance with Forearm Guarding Block
6. Pattern: Dan Gun
7. Three-Step Sparring Sequences 1-4

## *Yellow Belt Symbolism*

The colour yellow symbolizes the earth upon which seeds have been planted and are just beginning to sprout and form roots. Here a solid bedrock of TaeKwonDo basics is being laid.

## *Sambo Matsoki (Three-Step Sparring)*

**Sambo Matsoki or Three-Step sparring, is an exercise which allows beginning students to practice the basic TaeKwonDo techniques. This exercise is invaluable as it teaches a number of important concepts such as maintaining proper distance, facing the right direction, executing blocks, holding each stance correctly, accurate timing, and how to perform a counter attack.**

**When practicing the Three-Step style sparring, the attacker should assume a walking style stance and execute three middle section forward punches. They should also begin the series by stepping their right leg backwards paired with a low section block. The defender begins in a parallel ready stance.**

*First Sequence:*

Attack: Bring the right leg backwards into a walking stance. Pair this with a middle section inner block with the forearm repeated three times.

Defense: Counter attack using a reverse punch.

*Second Sequence:*

*Attack:* Move the left leg backwards to discover L-stance. Perform a middle section inner block with the forearm repeated three times.

*Defense:* Move your left leg forward and rotated 45 degrees. Then moving the right leg so that it lands behind the left leg of your opponent simultaneously creating a left oriented L-stance. Finally, perform a right knife-hand strike oriented towards the opponent's neck.

*Third Sequence:*

*Attack:* Perform an inside block with the forearm repeated three times.

*Defense:* Move forward into a left side L-Stance then perform a right forward backfist strike towards the opponent's face.

*Fourth Sequence:*

*Attack:* Move the left leg backwards into an L-stance. Complete a middle section inside block with the forearm oriented towards the outside and repeated three times.

*Defense:* Counter attack by arranging your left leg to create a sitting stance. Focus with your left hand before performing a double style punch.

## *Terminology*

| **Korean** | **Translation** |
|---|---|
| - Doong Joomuk | Back-fist |
| - An/aero | Inward/Inner |
| - Doong Joomuk Taerigi | Back-fist Strike |
| - Sonkal | Knife-hand (Shape) |
| - Sonkal Daebi-Makgi | Knife-hand (Shape) Guarding Style Block |
| - Sonkal Taerigi | Knife-hand Strike |
| - Bakaero | Outward (Direction) |
| - Sonbadak | Palm |
| - Ban-Javoo Matsoki | Semi Free-Sparring |
| - Yop Chajirugi | Side Piercing (Motion) Kick |
| - Sang Palmok Makgi | Twin (Outer) Forearm Block (Dan Gun) |

# Yellow Belt Pattern: Dan Gun

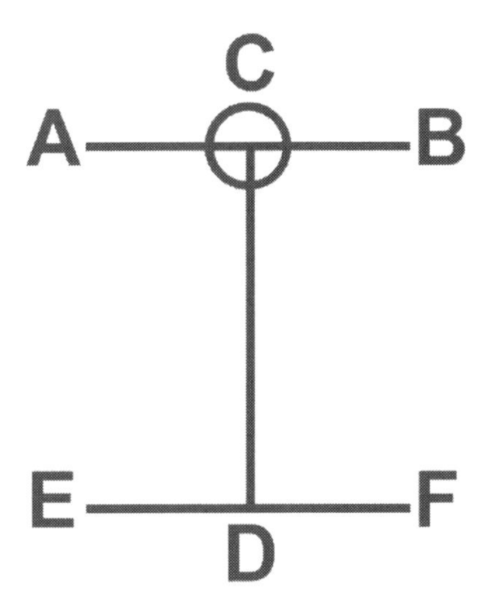


*The Dan Gun pattern takes its name from the holy Dan-Gun. It is said that he founded Korea in 2,333 BC. The pattern is made up of 21 movements and begins in the parallel ready stance.*

*Start:*

1. Bring your left foot towards B, creating a right side L-Stance oriented in the direction of B. Pair this with a middle section guarding knife-hand block also in the direction of B.

2. Step your right foot towards B, creating a right walking stance oriented in the direction of B. Complete a right high section punch also in the direction of B.

3. Work the right foot towards A, while rotating toward the right to create a left L-stance oriented in the direction of A. Perform a middle section knife-hand guarding block also in the direction of A.

4. Bring your left foot towards A, creating a left side walking stance oriented in the direction of A. Pair this with a left high section punch also in the direction of A.

5. Step your left foot towards D, creating a left side walking stance oriented in the direction of D. Complete a left low section forearm block also in the direction of D.

6. Work your right foot towards D, creating a right walking stance oriented in the direction of D. Perform a right high section punch also in the direction of D.

7. Bring your left foot towards D, creating a left side walking stance oriented in the direction of D. Pair this with a left high section punch also in the direction of D.

8. Step your right foot towards D, creating a right walking stance oriented in the direction of D. Complete a right high section punch also in the direction of D.

9. Work your left foot towards E while rotating towards the left, creating a right L-stance oriented in the direction of E. Perform a twin block with the forearms also in the direction of E.

10. Bring your right foot towards E, creating a right walking stance oriented in the direction of E. Pair this with a right high section punch also in the direction of E.

11. Step your right foot towards F, while rotating towards the right to create a left side L-Stance oriented in the direction of F. Complete a twin block with the forearms also in the direction of F.

12. Work your left foot towards F, creating a left side walking stance oriented in the direction of F. Perform a left high section punch also in the direction of F.

13. Bring your left foot towards C, creating a left side walking stance oriented in the direction of C. Pair this with a left low section forearm block also in the direction of C. Continue through movement 14 without pause.

14. Complete a left rising forearm block while holding a left side walking stance oriented in the direction of C.

15. Work your right foot towards C, creating a right walking stance oriented in the direction of C. Pair this with a right rising forearm block.

16. Bring your left foot towards C, creating a left side walking stance oriented in the direction of C. Complete a left rising forearm block.

17. Step your right foot towards C, creating a right waking stance oriented in the direction of C. Perform a right rising forearm block.

18. Work your left foot towards B while rotating towards the left to create a right L-stance oriented in the direction of B. Pair this with a left middle section outside knife-hand strike.

19. Bring your right foot towards B, creating a right walking stance oriented in the direction of B. Complete a right high section punch also in the direction of B.

20. Step your right foot towards A while rotating towards the right, creating a left L-stance oriented in the direction of A. Perform a right middle section outside knife-hand strike.

21. Work your left foot towards A, creating a left side walking stance oriented in the direction of A. Pair this with a left high section punch also in the direction of A.

*Finish the pattern by bringing your left foot backward into ready posture.

# Green Stripe Belt (Seventh Kup)

## *Requirements:*

1. Walking Stance with Back Fist Side Strike
2. Turning Kick with Knife-hand Guarding Block
3. Walking Stance with Wedging Block
4. Side Kick with Guarding Block
5. Walking Stance with Straight Spear Fingertip Thrust
6. Pattern: Do San
7. Three-Step Sparring Sequences 5-7

## *Green Belt Symbolism*

The plants which had begun to sprout at the yellow level are now growing alongside the student's new TaeKwonDo techniques.

## *Sambo Matsoki (Three-Step Sparring)*

**When practicing Three-Step sparring, the attacker should assume a walking stance and execute three middle section forward punches. They should also begin the series by stepping their right leg backwards, pairing the position with a low section block. The defender should begin in a parallel ready stance.**

*Fifth Sequence:*

*Attack:* Move your right leg backwards into an L-stance. Perform a middle outer block with your forearm repeated twice to the inside.

*Defense:* Move towards the right to create a sitting stance oriented parallel to the opponent. Complete a left outside block with your forearm paired with a high punch.

*Fifth Sequence:*

*Attack:* Move your right leg backwards to create an L-stance. Perform a middle  knife-hand style block, repeated twice to the inside.

*Defense:* Move towards the right to create a sitting stance oriented parallel to your opponent. Use a left outside knife-hand guard paired with a high section inward knife-hand strike towards the opponent's neck.

*Sixth Sequence:*

*Attack:* Move your left leg backwards to create an L-stance. Perform a middle section outer block with the forearm twice towards the inside.

*Defense:* Move the right foot to meet the left, push from the left and slide backwards along a 45 degree angle to create a right side L-Stance. Complete a guarding block with the forearm followed by a right front kick. Come down into a right walking stance paired with a double punch.

## *Terminology*

| **Korean** | **Translation** |
| --- | --- |
| - Sonkut | Fingertips |
| - Gojong Sogi | Fixed Stance |
| - Jayoo Matsoki | Free Sparring |
| - Sun | Straight (Shape) |
| - Sun Sonkut Tulgi | Straight (shaped) Fingertip Thrust |
| - Tulgi | Thrusting |

| | |
|---|---|
| - Dollyo Chagi | Turning Kick |
| - Hechvo Makgi | Wedging Style Block |
| - Jappyosol Tae | Wrist Release |

# Green Stripe Belt Pattern: Do San

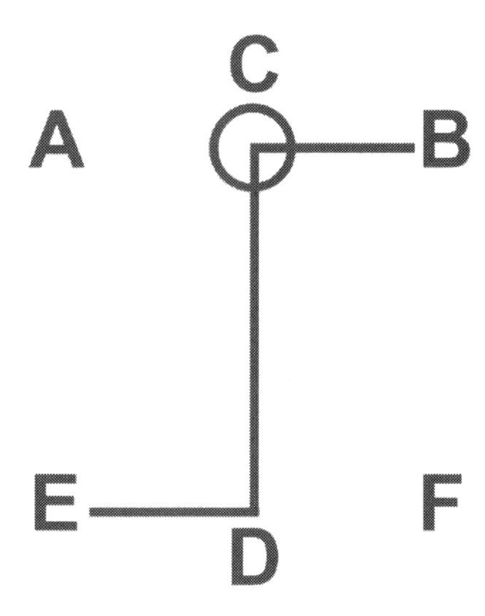


**The Do San pattern is an ode to a Korean patriot named Ahn Chang Ho. The 24 movements which make up the pattern are said to mimic events within his life which spanned from 1876 to 1938. During that time he was dedicated to developing education within Korea, and to its quest towards independence.**

***Start:*** The pattern begins in parallel ready stance.

1. Bring your left foot towards B, creating a left side walking stance oriented in the direction of B. Perform a high section outside forearm block also in the direction of B.

2. Complete a right middle section punch towards B while holding the left side walking stance still oriented in the direction of B.

3. Step your left foot along the AB line. Rotate towards the right, creating a right walking stance oriented in the direction of A. Pair this with a right outside high section forearm block also in the direction of A.

4. Perform a left middle section punch towards A, while holding the right walking stance also in the direction of A.

5. Bring your left foot towards D, creating a right L-stance oriented in the direction of D. Pair this with a middle section knife-hand style guarding block also in the direction of D.

6. Work your right foot towards D, creating a right walking stance in the direction of D. Complete a right middle section straight fingertip thrust towards D.

7. Rotate your body towards the left, also moving the right knife-hand until the palm of your hand is directed down towards the ground. Bring your left foot towards D and rotate towards the left, creating a left side walking stance oriented in the direction of D. Pair this with a left high section backfist strike.

8. Step your right foot towards D, creating a right walking stance oriented in the direction of D. Perform a right high section side backfist strike also in the direction of D.

9. Bring your left foot towards E while rotating to the left, creating a left side walking stance oriented in the direction of E. Complete a left high section outer forearm block also in the direction of E.

10. Perform a right middle section punch towards E while holding the left side walking stance also oriented in the direction of E.

11. Work your left foot towards the left along the EF line. Rotate to the right, creating a right walking stance oriented in the direction of F. Perform a right high section outside forearm block also in the direction of F.

12. Perform a left middle section punch towards F, while holding the right walking stance oriented in the direction of F.

13. Step your left foot towards the CE line, creating a left side walking stance oriented towards CE. Pair this with a high section outer wedging block with your forearm also in the direction of CE.

14. Complete a right middle section front snap style kick towards CE, while holding the same hand position as described in movement 13.

15. Bring your right foot down towards CE, creating a right walking stance oriented in the direction of CE. Perform a right middle section punch also in the direction of CE. Complete movements 15 and 16 fast and without pause.

16. Perform a left middle section punch towards CE, while holding the right waking stance facing CE.

17. Work your right foot towards CF, creating a right walking stance oriented in the direction of CF. Complete a high section outer wedging style block also in the direction of CF.

18. Perform a left middle section front snap kick towards CF, while holding the same hand position utilized in movement 17.

19. Bring your left foot down to meet the CF line and create a left side walking stance oriented in the direction of CF. Pair this with a left middle section punch also in the direction of CF. Complete movements 19 and 20 quickly and without pause.

20. Complete a right middle section punch towards CF, while holding the left side walking stance in the direction of CF.

21. Step your left foot towards C, creating a left side walking stance oriented in the direction of C. Pair this with a left rising forearm block.

22. Work your right foot towards C, creating a right walking stance oriented in the direction of C. Perform a right rising forearm block.

23. Bring your left foot towards B and rotate to the left, creating a sitting stance oriented in the direction of D. Complete a left middle section knife-hand side strike in the direction of B.

24. Step your left foot towards your right foot. Work your right foot towards A, creating a sitting stance oriented in the direction of D. Perform a right middle section knife-hand side strike in the direction of A.

*Finish the pattern by moving your right foot backward into the ready posture.

# Green Belt (Sixth Kup)

## *Requirements:*

1. Pattern: Won Hyo
2. 3-Step Sparring Sequences 8-10
3. Semi-Free Style Sparring Skills at the Basic Level
4. Combinations Based on the Patterns
5. Pattern: Designated by Exam Official

## *Green Belt Symbolism*

The plants which had begun to sprout at the yellow level are now growing alongside the student's new set of TaeKwonDo techniques.

## *Sambo Matsoki (3-Step Sparring)*

**When practicing the 3-Step style sparring, the attacker should assume a walking style stance and execute three middle section forward punches. They should also begin the series by stepping their Right-Side Leg backwards, pairing this position with a low section block. The defender begins in a parallel ready stance.**

*Seventh Sequence:*

*Attack:* Bring your Right-Side Leg backward into an L-stance. Repeat a middle knife-hand block twice towards the inside.

*Defense:* Counter attack by bringing your right foot towards the left. Push off from the left foot while sliding backwards and 45 degrees, creating a right L-stance. Pair this with a guarding forearm block. Complete a right side kick then come down into a left-side L-stance. Perform a knife-hand strike towards your opponent's neck or right forward backfist strike.

*Eighth Sequence:*

*Attack:* Move your Right-Side Leg backwards into an L-stance. Repeat a middle section palm style pushing block three times towards the outside.

*Defense:* Shift your body back in a 45 degree angle to create a Right-Side L-stance and bring your body to the outside of the opponent. Pair this with a knife-hand guarding block. Perform a right middle section turning kick, brining your kicking foot behind your opponent's front foot and coming down into a vertical style stance. Complete a knife-hand strike towards your opponent's neck.

*Ninth Sequence:*

*Attack:* Bring your Right-Side Leg backwards into an L-stance. Repeat a middle section knife-hand block twice towards the inside.

*Defense:* Work your right foot towards the left, then push from the left foot while sliding backwards along a 45 degree angle. Land in a Right-Side L-stance paired with a knife-hand guarding block. Perform a Reverse Side (Back) Kick then come down into a Right-side Walking stance. Pair this with a left reverse knife-hand strike towards the philtrum.

## *Banjayoo Matsoki (3-Step Semi-Free Sparring)*

In Banjayoo Matsoki or three-step semi-free sparring, the attacker should begin with one of their legs pressed backwards from L-stance paired with a guarding block. The defender begins in parallel stance. At the basic level, the attack consists of kicking first with the student's hind leg followed by a side kick and a turning kick. The defense consists of the proper block according to the kick used by the attacker. A counter attack should include a reverse punch.

## *Terminology*

| **Korean** | **Translation** |
|---|---|
| - Ibo Matoski | Two-Step Style Sparring |
| - Dwit | Back (Area) |
| - Dwit-Chook | Back Section Heel (Area of foot) |
| - Dwit-Kumchi | Back Section Sole (Area of foot) |
| - Goburvo Sogi | Bending Ready Stance |
| - Mao Chunbi Sogi - A | Closed Ready Stance Style: A |
| - Han-bansin | Parts of the Foot |
| - Sang-bansin | Parts of the Hand |
| - Golcho Makgi | Hooking Block |
| - Morup Chagi | Knee Strike |
| - Bandae-Dollyo Chagi | Reverse (Direction) Turning Kick |
| - Yop Jirugi | Side Punch |
| - Sewo Jirugi | Vertical Punch |

# Green Belt Pattern: Wun Hyo

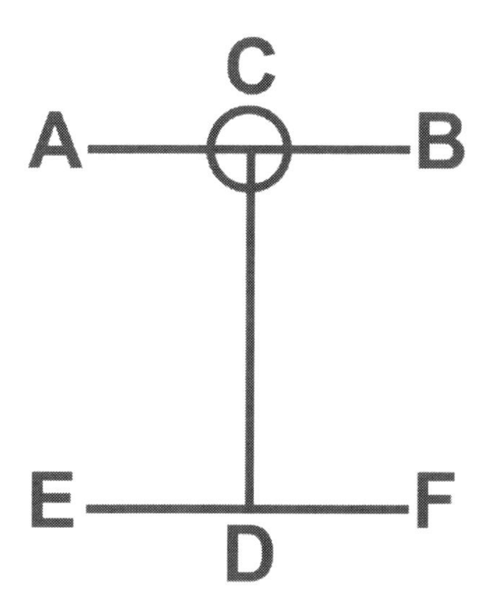


**The green-belt level Wun Hyo pattern is named after a monk. He is credited with introducing Buddhism to members of the Korean Silla Dynasty during 686 AD. The pattern is made up of 28 movements and begins in a closed position ready stance "A".**

*Start: Ready Stance 'A'*

1. Bring your left foot towards B, creating a right L-stance oriented in the direction of B. Complete a twin block with the forearm.

2. Perform a right high knife-hand strike inward towards B. Meanwhile move your left fist to the front near your right side shoulder. Hold a right side L-Stance oriented in the direction of B.

3. Complete a left mid-section punch towards B. Pair this with a left fixed stance oriented in the direction of B, while sliding your left foot towards B as well.

4. Move your right foot towards the right before shifting your right foot towards A, creating a left  L-stance oriented in the direction of A. Complete a twin block with the forearms.

5. Perform a left high knife-hand strike inward in the direction of A. Move your right first forward so it rests in front of your left shoulder. Hold a left side L-Stance towards A.

6. Complete a right mid-section punch towards A. Create a right fixed stance also in the direction of A. Move your right foot towards A as well.

7. Move your right foot towards the left. Rotate towards D to create a right bending ready stance "A" in the direction of D.

8. Perform a left mid-section side (piercing) kick towards D.

9. Bring your left foot down and towards D, creating a right side L-Stance oriented in the direction of D. Complete a mid-section knife-hand guarding block also in the direction of D.

10. Bring your right foot towards D, creating a left side L-Stance oriented in the direction of D. Perform a knife-hand guarding block also in the direction of D.

11. Work your left foot towards D, creating a right side L-Stance oriented towards D. Complete a mid-section knife-hand guarding block also in the direction of D.

12. Shift your right foot towards D, creating a right walking stance oriented in the direction of D. Pair this with a right mid-section straight fingertip thrust also in the direction of D.

13. Bring your left leg towards E while rotating to the left, creating a right side L-Stance oriented towards E. Perform a twin block with your forearms.

14. Complete a high inward right knife-hand strike towards E. Bring your left fist forward and beyond your right shoulder. Hold a right side L-Stance oriented in the direction of E.

15. Perform a left mid-section punch towards E, while creating a left fixed stance oriented in the direction of E and sliding your left foot towards E.

16. Move your left foot towards the right before moving your right foot towards F, creating a left side L-Stance oriented in the direction of F. Pair this with a twin block using your forearms.

17. Complete a left high inward knife-hand strike towards F. Move your right fist forward and beyond the left shoulder while holding a left side L-Stance oriented in the direction of F.

18. Perform a right mid-section punch towards F, creating a right fixed stance oriented in the direction of F. Slide your right foot towards F.

19. Move your right foot towards the left before moving your left foot towards C, creating a left side walking stance oriented in the direction of C. Perform a right circular inner forearm block towards CF.

20. Complete a right low section front snap kick toward C, while holding the hand position utilized in movement 19.

21. Bring your right foot down towards C, creating a right walking stance oriented in the direction of C. Perform a left mid-section punch towards C.

22. Perform a left circular inner forearm block towards CE, while holding a right walking stance oriented in the direction of C.

23. Complete a left low section front snap kick towards C, while holding the hands in the same position used in movement 22.

24. Bring your left foot down towards C, creating a left side walking stance oriented in the direction of C. Complete a right mid-section punch also towards C.

25. Rotate your face in the direction of C, creating a left bending ready stance "A" oriented in the direction of C.

26. Perform a right mid-section piercing kick towards C.

27. Bring your right foot down along CD. Shift your left foot towards B, rotating towards the left to create a right side L-Stance oriented in the direction of B. Pair this with a mid-section guarding block also towards B.

28. Move your left foot towards the right before moving your right foot towards B, creating a left L-stance oriented in the direction of A. Pair this with a mid-section guarding block towards A.

* Finish the pattern by moving your right foot backwards into ready posture.

# Blue Stripe Belt (Fifth Kup)

## *Requirements:*

1. Combinations Based on Patterns
2. Pattern: Student's Choice ( Not Including Yul Gok)
3. Pattern: Designated By Testing Official
4. Pattern: Yol Gok
5. Two-Step Sparring Sequences 1-4
6. Semi-Free Sparring Skills at the Intermediate Level
7. Free Style Sparring Skills Techniques

## *Blue Belt Symbolism*

The blue coloured belt symbolizes the plants as they transform into tall trees with limbs reaching towards the heavens. Likewise, the student's TaeKwonDo knowledge and skills mature.

## *Ibo Matsoki (Two-Step Sparring)*

When Ibo Matsoki or Two-Step style sparring is practiced at the intermediate level it reinforces the advanced techniques of TaeKwonDo. It utilizes the same theories of time and distancing as practiced in Three-Step style sparring paired with a new range of attacks. As a result the student acquires a variety of combinations.

The attacker begins with their right leg positioned towards the back paired with a forearm guarding block. The defender should begin in a parallel ready stance.

*Sequence One*

*Attack:* Perform a high section punch paired with a front section kick.

*Defense:* Move your left leg backwards into a walking stance paired with a rising block. Move your right leg backwards to form a waking stance paired with an X-fist pressing block.

*Counter Attack:* Initiate a twin vertical section punch.

*Sequence Two*

*Attack:* Perform a side section punch in a fixed stance followed by a turning kick.

*Defense:* Move your right leg backward to create an L-stance before performing an upward palm block. Move your left leg backward into an L-stance followed by a waist block.

*Counter Attack:* Shift towards the front to create a right side L-Stance paired with a right side elbow blow.

*Sequence Three*

*Attack:* Perform a front kick paired with a twin vertical punch.

*Defense:* Move your right leg backwards into a walking stance. Perform an X-fist pressing block. Move your left leg backwards into a walking stance paired with an outer wedging block with your forearm.

Counter Attack: Initiate a knee kick paired with a pull to your opponent's shoulders.

*Sequence Four*

*Attack:* Perform a flat fingertip thrust paired with a side kick.

Defense: Move your right leg backwards into a walking stance. Perform a knife-hand rising block. Move your left leg back into an L-stance and perform an inside palm block.

*Counter Attack:* Perform a front kick towards your opponent's coccyx followed by a twin upset punch towards your opponent's kidneys.

## *Ban Jayoo Matsoki (Three-Step Semi-Free Sparring)*

In Ban Jayoo Matsoki or three-step semi-free style sparring, the attacker should begin with one of their legs pressed backwards from L-stance with a guarding block. The defender begins in a parallel stance. At the intermediate level the attacker first performs a front, side, turning, or reverse side kick with their hind leg. The defense performs whichever block corresponds with the attacker's kick. A counter attack should involve striking with the hands.

## *Terminology*

| **Korean** | **Translation** |
|---|---|
| - Sonkut | Fingertips |
| - Gojong Sogi | Fixed Stance |
| - Jayoo Matsoki | Free Sparring |
| - Sun | Straight |
| - Sun Sonkut Tulgi | Straight Fingertip Thrust |
| - Tulgi | Thrust |
| - Dollyo Chagi | Turning Kick |
| - Hechvo Makgi | Wedging Block |
| - Jappyosol-Tae | Wrist Release |

# Blue Stripe Belt Pattern: Yul Gok

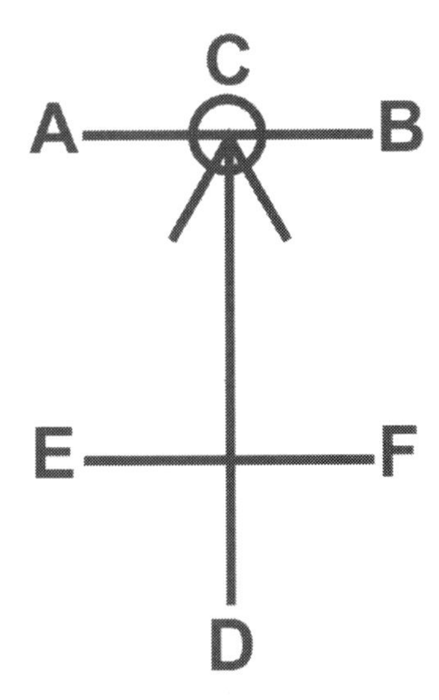


**The Yul Gok pattern is named in tribute to a scholar and philosopher by the name of Yi l. This great man lived from 1536 to 1584 and to some is considered the "Confucius of Korea". The pattern consists of 38 movements. This number is significant as it nods to the 38th latitude where Yi l was born. The diagram utilized also symbolizes the "scholar".**

***Start:*** The student should begin the pattern in a parallel ready stance.

1. Bring your left foot towards B, creating a sitting stance oriented in the direction of D. Meanwhile send your left fist towards D.

2. Reaffirm the sitting stance oriented towards D then perform a right middle section punch towards D. Continue through movement 3 without pause.

3. Find the sitting stance oriented in the direction of D again, then complete a left middle section punch also towards D.

4. Move your left foot towards the right. Next, move the right foot towards A, creating a sitting stance oriented in the direction of D. Send your right fist towards D.

5. Reaffirm the sitting stance oriented in the direction of D, then perform a left middle section punch towards D. Continue through movement 6 quickly and without pause.

6. Find a sitting stance oriented in the direction of D before completing a right middle section punch also in the direction of D.

7. Bring your right foot towards AD, creating a right walking stance oriented in the direction of AD. Perform a right middle section inner forearm block also in the direction of AD.

8. Complete a left low section front snap kick towards AD while maintaining the hand positioning utilized in movement 7.

9. Bring your left leg down towards AD, creating a left side walking stance oriented in the direction of AD. Perform a left middle section punch also in the direction of AD. Continue through movement 10 quickly and without pause.

10. Discover a left side walking stance oriented in the direction of AD before completing a right middle section punch also in the direction of AD.

11. Bring your left foot towards BD, creating a left side walking stance oriented in the direction of BD. Perform a left middle section inner forearm block also towards BD.

12. Complete a right low section forward snap kick towards BD, while maintaining the same hand position utilized in movement 11.

13. Drop your right foot down towards BD, creating a right walking stance oriented in the direction of BD. Perform a right middle section punch also in the direction of BD. Continue through movement 14 quickly and without pause.

14. Maintain the right walking stance as you initiate a left middle section punch towards BD.

15. Complete a right middle section hooking block towards D, moving into a right waking stance oriented in the direction of D, while pivoting your left foot.

16. Continue to hold the right walking stance oriented in the direction of D as you perform a left middle section hooking block also towards D. Continue through movement 17 quickly and without pause.

17. Hold the right walking stance oriented in the direction of D and complete a right middle section punch also towards D.

18. Work your left foot towards D, creating a left side walking stance oriented in the direction of D. Perform a left middle section hooking block also towards D.

19. Hold the left side walking stance oriented in the direction of D while you complete a right middle section hooking block also towards D. Continue through movement 20 quickly and without pause.

20. Continue to hold the left side walking stance oriented in the direction of D as you perform a left middle section punch towards D.

21. Shift your right foot towards D, creating a right walking stance oriented in the direction of D. Perform a right middle section punch also towards D.

22. Rotate until you are facing in the direction of D, thus creating a right bending ready stance" A" oriented in the direction of D.

23. Perform a left middle section side piercing kick towards D.

24. Bring your left foot down towards D, creating a left side walking stance oriented in the direction of D. Strike the left palm with the front of your right elbow.

25. Rotate until you are facing in the direction of C, thus creating a left bending ready stance "A" oriented in direction of C.

26. Perform a right middle section side piercing kick.

27. Bring your right foot down towards C, creating a right walking stance oriented in the direction of C. Strike the right palm with the front of your right elbow.

28. Shift your left foot towards E, creating a right side L-Stance oriented in the direction of E. Pair this with a twin knife-hand block.

29. Step your right foot towards E, creating a right walking stance oriented in the direction of E. Perform a right middle section thrust with straight finger tips as also towards E.

30. Bring your right foot towards F, rotate to the right, creating a left side L-Stance oriented in the direction of F. Pair this with a twin knife-hand block.

31. Shift your right foot towards F, creating a left side walking stance oriented in the direction of F. Perform a left middle section thrust with straight finger tips also towards F.

32. Step your left foot towards C, creating a left side walking stance oriented in the direction of C. Pair this with a left high section outer forearm block also towards C.

33. Continue to hold the left side walking stance oriented in the direction of C while you perform a right middle section punch also towards C.

34. Bring your right foot towards C, creating a right walking stance oriented in the direction of C. Pair this with a right high section outer side block with your forearm.

35. Hold the right walking stance oriented in the direction of C while you perform a left middle section punch also towards C.

36. Execute a jump towards C, creating a left X-stance oriented in the direction of B. Complete a left high section side back strike also towards C.

37. Step your right foot towards A, creating a right walking stance oriented in the direction of A. Perform a right high section double forearm block also towards A.

38. Move your right foot towards the left before shifting your left foot towards B, creating a left side walking stance oriented in the direction of B. Pair this with a left high section double forearm block also towards B.

* Finish the pattern by moving your left foot backwards into ready posture.

# Blue Belt (Fourth Kup)

## *Requirements:*

1. Pattern: Chosen By the Student ( Not Including Joong-Gun)
2. Pattern: Designated By Testing Official
3. Pattern: Joong Gun
4. Two-Step Sparring Sequences 5-8
5. Three-Step Semi-Free Sparring Skills at the Advanced Level
6. Padwork Skills
7. Free Sparring Skills

## *Blue Belt Symbolism*

The blue coloured belt symbolizes the plants as they transform into tall trees with limbs reaching towards the heavens. Likewise, the student's TaeKwonDo knowledge and skills mature.

## *Ibo Matsoki (Two-Step Sparring)*

The attacker begins with their right-side Leg positioned towards the back paired with a forearm guarding block. The defender should begin in a parallel position ready stance.

*First Sequence*

*Attack:* Perform a right back kick while in the left side walking stance followed by a high section palm strike.

*Defense:* Assume the right-side L-stance paired with a palm waist section block. Discover a left side L-Stance paired with an inward outer section forearm block.

*Counter Attack:* Assume the right walking stance and perform a left reverse knife-hand blow followed with a middle section inward strike sliding your right foot.

*Second Sequence*

*Attack:* Perform a high section turning kick in the left side walking stance followed by an arc-hand strike.

*Defense:* Assume sitting stance paired with twin parallel forearm blocks while sliding your left foot in a diagonal direction. Assume a right-side L-stance with a Palm Hook block, grasping your opponent's arm.

*Counter Attack:* Initiate a left position side kick while holding on to your opponent's arm.

*Third Sequence*

*Attack:* Assume a right, fixed stance and perform a side fist strike followed be a left middle section reverse turning kick.

Defense: Assume a left side L-Stance paired with a twin forearm block. Move into a right-side L-stance and perform a knife-hand style guarding block while gliding away.

Counter Attack: Assume a left X-stance paired with a high section backfist side strike.

## *Ban Jayoo Matsoki (Three-Step Semi-Free Sparring)*

In Ban Jayoo Matsoki the attacker begins in an L-stance paired with a guarding block. They should initiate each attack with one of their legs stepped backwards. Meanwhile the defender should begin in parallel stance.

At the advanced level the attacker takes a step forward and repeats each technique three times. The proper defense includes the block which corresponds with the technique being used. In the counter attack phase any hand or foot technique may be used.

## *Pad Work*

This allows the student to practice measuring their intentions and executing kicks. Students should practice their side kick, turning kick, side kick, reverse side kick, and reverse turning kick.

## *Free Sparring*

This practice is used to allow students to practice their training. Here there are no preordained sequences, therefore a student will not know what kind of attack to prepare for. As a result you will not see as great of a variety of defense techniques used as you might expect in other sparring methods. This is strictly a no-contact practice, eliminating the need for pads. However, if the students or instructor should choose to participate in semi-contact sparring proper protection and supervision will need to be available to ensure student safety.

## *Terminology*

| **Korean** | **Translation** |
|---|---|
| - Bandal Sun | Arc-Hand |
| - Duit Chaqi | Back Kick |
| - Moa Junbu Sogi "B" | Closed Ready Stance style: B |
| - Yonsok Chagi | Consecutive Kick |
| - Naervo Makgi | Downward Block |
| - Naervo Chagi | Downward Kick |
| - Dollyon Joo | Forging Post |
| - Nachuo Sogi | Low Stance |

| | |
|---|---|
| - Ilbo Matsoki | One-Step Sparring |
| - Noolloo Chagi | Pressing style Kick |
| - Noolloo Makgi | Pressing Block |
| - Dwit-Bal Sogi | Rear-Foot Stance (Joong Gun) |
| - Bandae Dollyo Goro Chagi | Reverse Turning Hooking |
| - Duro Makgi | Scooping (motion) Block |
| - Yop-Bal Badack | Side-Sole (area of foot) |
| - Dollyo Jirugi | Turning (motion) Punch |
| - YopCha Tulgi | Side Thrusting (motion) Kick |
| - Sang-Dwijibo Jirugi | Twin Upset Punch (Joong Gun) |
| - Wi Palkup Taeregi | Upper Elbow Strike |
| - Kyocha Makgi | X-Block |

# Blue Belt Pattern: Joong Gun

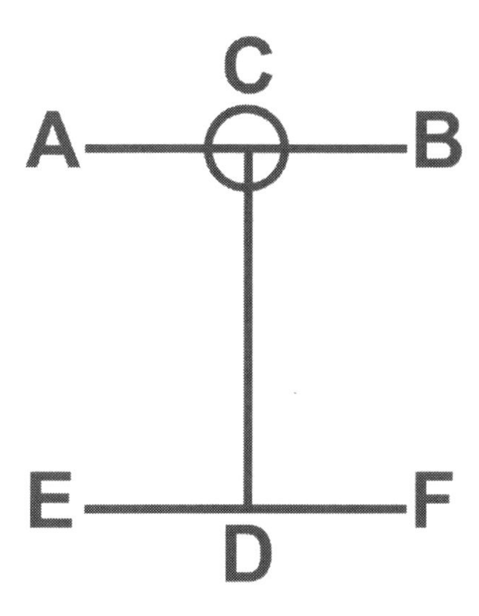


**The Joong Gun pattern was named for Ahn Joong-Gun, a Korean patriot. He is most known for having assassinated Hiro-Bumi who was the premier Japanese governor and general for Korea. He also played a vital role in the Korean-Japanese merger. The pattern is made up of 32 movements which serve to signify the age at which Ahn Joong-Gun was put to death inside the Lui-Shung prison during 1910.**

***Start:*** Begin the pattern in a closed ready stance "B".

1. Bring your left foot towards B, creating a right side L-Stance oriented in the direction of B. Pair this with a left middle section reverse knife-hand block also towards B.

2. Perform a left low section side front snap kick towards B while maintaining the same hand positioning as utilized in movement 1.

3. Bring your left foot down towards B before moving your right foot also towards B, creating a left rear foot stance oriented in the direction of B. Pair this with a right upward section block with the palm.

4. Step your right foot towards A, creating a left side L-Stance oriented in the direction of A. Pair this with a right middle section reverse knife-hand block also towards A.

5. Maintain the same hand positioning utilized in movement 4, as you initiate a right low section side front snap kick in the direction of A.

6. Bring your right foot down towards A before shifting your left foot towards A to create a right rear foot stance oriented in the direction of A. Perform a left upward section palm block.

7. Shift your left leg towards D, creating a right side L-Stance oriented in the direction of D. Pair this with a middle section knife-hand guarding block towards D.

8. Complete a right upper section elbow strike, meanwhile creating a left side walking stance oriented towards D before sliding your left foot also in the direction of D.

9. Bring your right foot towards D, creating a left side L-Stance oriented in the direction of D. Pair this with a middle knife-hand guarding block also towards D.

10. Complete a left upper section elbow strike, meanwhile creating a right walking stance oriented in the direction of D before sliding your right foot also towards D.

11. Bring your left foot towards D, creating a left side walking stance oriented in the direction of D. Perform  a twin high section vertical punch in the direction of D.

12. Step your right foot towards D, creating a right walking stance oriented in the direction of D. Complete a twin upset punch also towards D.

13. Shift your right foot along the CD line. Rotate towards the left to create a left side walking stance oriented in the direction of C. Perform an X-fist rising block.

14. Bring your left foot towards E, creating a right side L-Stance oriented in the direction of E. Complete a left high section side back strike also towards E.

15. Rotate your left fist towards the left so that it faces down. Assume a left side walking stance oriented in the direction of E. Then perform a left side walking stance also in the direction of E while sliding your left foot towards E. Continue through movement 16 quickly and without pause.

16. Hold the left side walking stance oriented in the direction of E and perform a right high section punch also towards E.

17. Move your left foot towards the right before shifting your right foot towards F, creating a left side L-Stance oriented in the direction of F. Initiate a right high section side back strike also towards F.

18. Rotate your right fist towards the right until your back fist is facing down and the rest of your body creates a right walking stance oriented in the direction of F, then slide your right foot towards F as well. Continue through movement 19 quickly and without pause.

19. Hold the right walking stance oriented in the direction of F while performing a left high section punch towards F.

20. Step your right foot towards the left before shifting your left foot towards C, creating a left side walking stance oriented in the direction of C. Initiate a left high section double forearm block also towards C.

21. Complete a left middle section punch towards C, meanwhile creating a right side L-Stance also oriented towards C.

22. Perform a right middle section side piercing kick towards C.

23. Bring your right foot down towards C, creating a right walking stance oriented in the direction of C. Pair this with a right high section double forearm block also towards C.

24. Complete a right middle section punch towards C meanwhile creating a left side L-Stance oriented towards C and pulling against your right foot.

25. Perform a left middle section side piercing kick towards C.

26. Bring your left foot down towards C, creating a right side L-Stance oriented in the direction of C. Pair this with a middle section forearm guarding block also towards C.

27. Slowly perform a right pressing palm block meanwhile creating a left low section stance oriented in the direction of C. Slide your left foot towards C.

28. Shift your right foot towards C, creating a left side L-Stance oriented in the direction of C. Pair this with a Middle section forearm guarding block also towards C.

29. Slowly complete a left palm pressing block, meanwhile creating aright low section stance oriented in the direction of C. Slide your right foot towards C.

30. Slowly shift your left foot towards your right, creating a closed stance oriented in the direction of A. Complete a right angle punch.

31. Bring your right foot towards A, creating a right fixed stance oriented in the direction of A. Pair this with a U-shape block also towards A.

32. Step your right foot towards your left before shifting your left foot towards B, creating a left fixed stance oriented in the direction of B. Pair this with a U-shape block also in the direction of B.

*Complete the pattern by moving your left foot backwards into ready posture.

# Red Stripe Belt (Third Kup)

## *Requirements:*

1. Pattern: The Students Choosing ( Not Including Toi Gye)
2. Pattern: Designated By the Test Official
3. Pattern: Toi Gye
4. Three-Step Semi-Free  Sparring Skills at the Advanced Level
5. One Step Sparring Skills at the Basic Level
6. Padwork Skills
7. Free Style Sparring Skills

### Red Belt Symbolism

The red coloured belt symbolizes both danger and caution. A student must master the ability to control their own actions. It also alerts an opponent to keep their distance.

## *Ilbo Matsoki (One Step Sparring)*

Since Ilbo Matsoki is intended to be practiced with each individual's unique ideas, the sequences listed below are purely to be used as a guide to create your own techniques. It is quite different from free sparring. To practice one step sparring begin with the previously studied Three-Step counter attack paired with the additional techniques described here.

The defender will need to develop quick reflexes to respond to the attack. Both participants should start in a parallel ready position unless instructed to do otherwise.

*First Sequence*

Begin in a parallel ready position. Move your right foot forward into a walking stance before initiating a right punch. During the second set, take another step forward with the left foot and initiate a left punch.

*Second Sequence*

Shift your left foot forward along a 45 degree angle. Step your right foot back so that it rests just behind your opponent's front leg and creating a left side L-Stance. Perform a knife-hand strike with your right arm aimed towards your opponent's neck. Finish with a right side kick before stepping away from your opponent.

*Third Sequence*

Assume a left side L-Stance before performing a right forward backfist style strike towards your opponent's face. Continue with a left upward punch and a right hooking punch.

*Fourth Sequence*

Bring your left foot into sitting stance.  Focus your left hand before performing a double punch and right turning kick. Finish with a left reverse side kick.

*Fifth Sequence*

Step to the right, creating a parallel sitting stance. Perform a left outside block with your forearm followed by a raised punch. Meanwhile, grasp your opponent's head in both of your hands. Finish with a left knee strike.

## *Pad Work Sparring Routine*

Between each kick, swap legs and perform a jump.

- Single 45 Kick
- Single 45 Kick
- Double 45 Kick

Practice these techniques, leading with either leg.

- High Section Instep Turning Kick
- Downward Axe Kick

## *Terminology*

| **Korean** | **Translation** |
|---|---|
| - Twimyo | - Flying (to fly in technique) |
| - Twimyo Chagi | - Flying Style Kick |
| - Ap-Cha Milgi | - Front Pushing Style Kick |
| - Digutia Makgi | - U-Shaped Block |
| - Dwijibun Sonkut | - Upset Fingertips |
| - San Makgi | - W-Shaped Block (Toi Gye) |
| - Doru-Chagi | - Waving Kick |

# Red Stripe Belt Pattern: Toi Gye

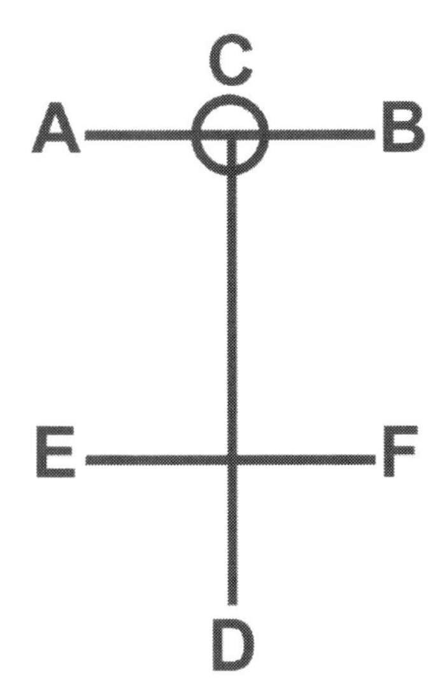


**The Toi Gye pattern was given the pen name of a noted scholar from the sixteenth century. The man's true identity is Yi Hwang and he was a noteworthy authority regarding Neo-Confucianism. This red belt pattern is made up of 37 movements, signifying the 37$^{th}$ latitude where he was born. In addition, the diagram used signifies "the scholar" as an additional tribute.**

*Start:* A student should begin the pattern in the closed ready stance "B".

1. Bring your left foot towards B, creating a right sided L Stance oriented in the direction of B. Pair this with an inner middle section forearm block also towards B.

2. Perform a right low section upset fingertip thrust towards B, meanwhile creating a left side walking stance oriented in the direction of B. Slide your left foot towards B.

3. Slowly step your left foot towards your right, creating a closed stance oriented in the direction of D. Initiate a right side back strike towards C, bringing your left arm down and to the side.

4. Bring your right foot towards A, creating a left sided L-stance oriented in the direction of A. Pair this with a right-side middle-section inner forearm block also towards A.

5. Perform a left low section upset finger tip thrust towards A, meanwhile creating a right-side walking stance oriented in the direction of A. Slide your right foot towards A as well.

6. Slowly step your right foot towards your left, creating a closed stance oriented in the direction of D. Initiate a left side back strike towards C, bringing your right arm down and to the side.

7. Shift your left foot towards D, creating a left side walking stance oriented in the direction of D. Pair this with an X-fist pressing block. Continue through movement 8 without a pause.

8. Hold the left side walking stance oriented in the direction of D and perform a twin high section vertical punch towards D.

9. Perform a right-side middle-section snap kick towards D, while maintaining the hand positioning utilized in movement 8.

10. Bring your right foot down towards D, creating a right-side walking stance oriented in the direction of D. Initiate a right-side middle-section punch towards D.

11. Hold the right-side walking stance oriented in the direction of D and perform a left middle section punch towards D.

12. Slowly step your left foot towards your right, creating a closed stance oriented in the direction of F. Initiate a twin side thrust with your elbow.

13. Stamp your right foot towards F, creating a sitting stance oriented in the direction of C. Pair this with a right outside W-shape forearm block.

14. Stamp your left foot towards F and rotate to the right, creating a sitting stance oriented in the direction of D. Perform a left outer W-shape forearm block towards D.

15. Stamp your left foot towards E and rotate towards the right, creating a sitting stance oriented in the direction of C. Perform a left outer W-shape forearm block in the direction of C.

16. Stamp your right foot towards E, and rotate to the left, creating a sitting stance oriented in the direction of D. Perform a right outer W-shape forearm block towards D.

17. Stamp your left foot towards E, and rotate to the right, creating a sitting stance oriented in the direction of C. Perform a left outer W-shape block towards C.

18. Stamp your left foot towards F, and rotate towards the right, creating a sitting stance oriented in the direction of D. Perform a left outer W-shape forearm block towards D.

19. Step your right foot towards your right before shifting your left foot towards D, creating a right sided L-stance oriented in the direction of D. Pair this with a double left low section pushing forearm block also towards D.

20. Stretch your hands up as though you were going to take hold of your opponent's head. Meanwhile adopt a left side walking stance oriented in the direction of D and slide your left foot towards D.

21. Perform a right upward knee kick and drop your hands down towards the floor.

22. Bring your right foot down towards your left foot before stepping your left foot towards C, creating a tight L-stance oriented in the direction of C. Pair this with a middle section knife-hand block also towards C.

23. Initiate a left low section side front snap style kick towards C while maintaining the same hand positioning utilized in movement 22.

24. Bring your left foot down towards C, creating a left side walking stance oriented in the direction of C. Perform a left high section left flat finger tip thrust towards C.

25. Step your right foot towards C, Creating a left side L-Stance oriented in the direction of C. Pair this with a middle section knife-hand block also towards C.

26. Initiate a right low section side front snap kick towards C while maintaining the same hand positioning utilized in movement 25.

27. Bring your right foot down towards C, creating a right-side walking stance oriented in the direction of C. Perform a right high section flat finger tip thrust also towards C.

28. Step your right foot towards D, creating a right side L-Stance oriented in the direction of C. Initiate a right side back strike towards D paired with a left low section forearm flock towards C.

29. Initiate a jump towards C, creating a right X-stance oriented in the direction of A. Pair this with an X-fist pressing block.

30. Bring your right foot towards C, creating a right-side walking stance oriented in the direction of C. Perform a right double high section forearm block also towards C.

31. Step your left foot towards B, creating a right side L-Stance oriented in the direction of B. Pair this with a low section knife-hand guarding block also towards B.

32. Perform a right circular inner forearm block towards BD while assuming a left side walking stance oriented in the direction of B and sliding your left foot towards B.

33. Step your left foot towards your right before shifting your right foot towards A, creating a left side L-Stance oriented in the direction of A. Pair this with a low section knife-hand guarding block also towards A.

34. Assume s right-side walking stance oriented in the direction of A and perform a left inner circular forearm block towards AD while sliding your right foot towards A.

35. Adopt a left side walking stance oriented in the direction of CE and perform a right inner circular forearm block also towards CE.

36. Adopt a right-side walking stance oriented in the direction of A and perform a left inner circular forearm block towards AD.

37. Bring your right foot upon the AB line, creating a sitting stance oriented in the direction of D. Initiate a right-side middle-section punch also towards D.

*Complete the pattern by moving your right foot backward into ready posture.

# Red Belt (Second Kup)

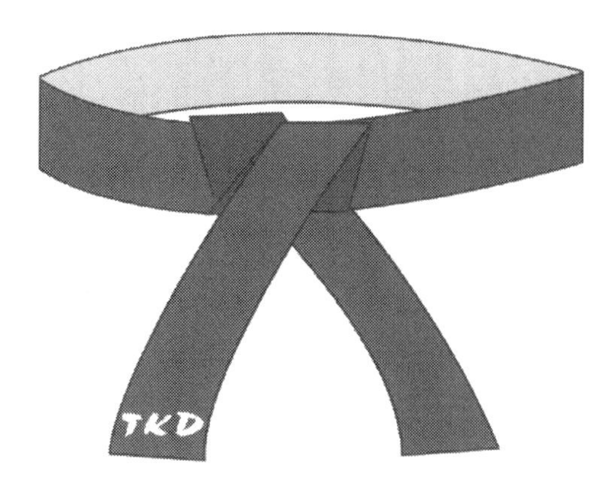


## *Requirements:*

1. Combinations based on Patterns
2. Pattern: Designated By Test Official
3. Pattern: Hwa-Rang
4. Three-Step Sparring Skills
5. Two-Step Sparring Skills
6. One-Step Sparring Skills
7. Padwork Skills
8. Free Style Sparring Skills

## *Red Belt Symbolism*

The red coloured belt symbolizes both danger and caution. A student must master the ability to control their own actions. It also alerts an opponent to keep their distance.

## *Ilbo Matsoki (One Step Sparring)*

At the red belt level, students will create their own one step sparring techniques. They should derive these techniques from the lessons and experiences they have had during their TaeKwonDo training. The attacker and defender both begin in the parallel ready position. The attacker takes a step with their right leg, creating a walking stance. Then they will initiate blows with their right hand. In the following scenario, the attacker will take a second step forward, this time with their left leg. Then they will initiate blows with their left hand. Below is a list of recommended applications involving Ilbo Matsoki, or one step sparring.

1. Only Use Hand
2. Only Use Foot
3. Use Hand & foot
4. Use Foot & hand
5. Add Jumping
6. Practice Lock & restraint

## *Focus Pad Work Sparring exercise*

Practice a single minute of various hand combinations working on 2 pads. Then practice a single minute of footwork with two pads.

## *Terminology*

| **Korean** | **Translation** |
| --- | --- |
| - Moa-chunbi Sogi "C" | - Closed Ready Stance Type: C |
| - Sunkut | - Fingertips |
| - Twimyo-Nopi Chagi | - Flying High Section Kick |
| - An | - Inside/Inner |
| - Baldung | - Instep (of foot) |
| - Bakat | - Outside/Outer |
| - Miro Makgi | - Pushing Block |
| - Baldal-Dung | - Reverse Footsword |
| - Hullyo Makgi | - Sweeping Style Block |
| - Sang-Bal Chagi | - Twin Footed Kick |
| - Bituro Chagi | - Twist Kick |
| - Ollyo-Jirugi | - Upward (Direction) Punch |
| - Sewo Chagi | - Vertical (Direction) Kick |

# Red Belt Pattern: Hwa Rang

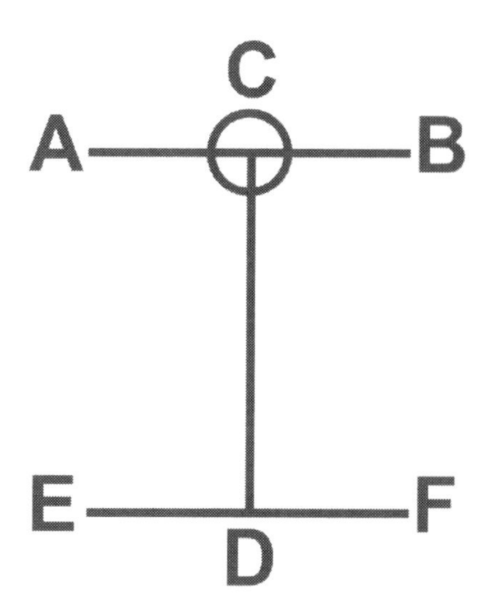


**The Hwa Rang pattern acts a tribute to the well-known Hwa-Rang youth group. The group was founded in 600 AD, during the Silla Dynasty. Later it would play an invaluable role in the unification of Korea's three kingdoms. It is made up of 29 movements which symbolize the 29th Infantry Division which allowed TaeKwonDo to mature and grow.**

***Start:*** Begin this red belt pattern in the closed ready stance "C".

1. Bring your left foot towards D, creating a sitting stance oriented in the direction of D. Pair this with a left side middle section pushing palm block also towards D.

2. Maintain the sitting stance oriented in the direction of D and perform a right middle section punch also towards D.

3. Continue the sitting stance oriented in the direction of D and initiate a left middle section punch also towards D.

4. Perform a twin block with your forearms meanwhile creating a left side L-Stance oriented in the direction of A, adding a pivot with your left foot.

5. Hold the left side L-Stance oriented in the direction of A and initiate a left upward punch meanwhile bringing your right fist to the front of your left shoulder.

6. Perform a right middle section punch towards A. Slide into a right fixed stance also in the direction of A.

7. Create a left side vertical stance oriented in the direction of A and initiate a right sided downward knifehand strike.

8. Bring your left foot towards A, creating a left side walking stance oriented in the direction of A. Perform a left middle section punch also towards A.

9. Step your left foot towards D, creating a left side walking stance oriented in the direction of D. Pair this with a left low section forearm block also towards D.

10. Bring your right foot towards D, creating a right walking stance oriented in the direction of D. Perform a right middle section punch also towards D.

11. Tug your left foot towards your right and move your left palm towards your right fist. Flex your right elbow at a 45 degree angle oriented outward.

12. Perform a right middle section side piercing kick towards D. Tug your hands in the opposite direction. Bring your leg down towards D, creating a left side L-Stance oriented in the direction of D. Initiate a right middle section outside knife-hand strike also towards D.

13. Bring your left foot towards D, creating a left side walking stance oriented in the direction of D. Perform a left middle section punch also towards D.

14. Step your right foot towards D, forming a right walking stance oriented in the direction of D. Initiate a right middle section punch also towards D.

15. Bring your left foot towards E and rotate to the left, creating a right side L-Stance oriented in the direction of E. Pair this with a middle section knife-hand guarding block also towards E.

16. Shift your right foot towards E, creating a right walking stance oriented in the direction of E. Perform a right middle section straight fingertip thrust also towards E.

17. Bring your right foot upon the EF line, creating a right side L-Stance oriented in the direction of F. Pair this with a middle section knife-hand guarding block towards E.

18. Perform a right high section turning kick towards DF before lowering your right foot towards F. Continue through movement 19 quickly and without pause.

19. Initiate a left high section turning kick towards CF. Bring your left foot down towards F, creating a right side L-Stance oriented in the direction of F. Pair this movement with a middle section knife-hand guarding block also towards F.

20. Bring your left foot towards C, creating a left side walking stance oriented in the direction of C. Perform a left low section forearm block also towards C.

21. Initiate a right middle section punch towards C, then assume a right side L-Stance oriented in the direction of C, while tugging on your left foot.

22. Bring your right foot towards C, creating a left side L-Stance oriented in the direction of C. Perform a left middle section punch also towards C.

23. Shift your left foot towards C, creating a right side L-Stance oriented in the direction of C. Initiate a right middle section punch also towards C.

24. Perform an X-fist pressing block, then assume a left side walking stance oriented in the direction of C, while also sliding your left foot towards C.

25. Slide your right foot towards C to create a right side L-Stance oriented in the direction of D. Perform a right side elbow thrust also towards C.

26. Step your left foot towards your right foot before rotating to the left, creating a closed stance oriented in the direction of B. Perform a right side front inner forearm block, reaching your left forearm down and toward the side.

27. Hold the closed stance in the direction of B and pair it with a left side front inner forearm block while reaching your right forearm down toward the side.

28. Shift your left foot towards B, creating an L-stance oriented in the direction of B. Pair this with a middle section knife-hand guarding block also towards B.

29. Step your left foot towards your right foot before shifting your right foot towards A, creating a left side L-Stance oriented in the direction of A. Pair this with a middle section knife-hand guarding block also towards A.

* Finish the pattern by moving your right foot backwards into the ready posture.

# Red Belt – Black Stripe (First Kup)

## *Requirements:*

1. Combinations based on Patterns
2. Pattern: Students Choice( Not Including Choong Moo)
3. Pattern: Designated By Test Official
4. Pattern: Choong Moo
5. Three-Step Sparring Skills
6. Two-Step Sparring Skills
7. One Step Sparring Skills at the Advanced Level
8. Free Style Sparring Skills

## *Black Belt Symbolism*

The black coloured belt exists in direct contrast to the white belt. This difference reflects the proficiency of a black belt practitioner in relation to the white belt beginner. In addition the black belt symbolizes the practitioners lack of fear regarding darkness or the unknown.

## *Terminology*

| *Korean* | *Translation* |
| --- | --- |
| - Momchau Makgi | Checking Block |
| - Doo-bandalson makgi | Double arc-hand block |
| - Nervo Makgi | Downward Block |
| - Opun Sonkut Tulgi | Flat Fingertip Thrust |
| - Wae-Bal Sogi | One Leg Stance |
| - Bakat | Outside/Outer |
| - Twyo Nomo Chagi | Overhead Kick |
| - Sonkul Dung | Reverse Knife-hand |
| - Hullyio Makgi | Side Fist |
| - Cha-Bapgi | Stamp-Kick |
| - Goreo-Chagi | Sweep-Kick |

# Red Belt - Black Stripe Pattern: Choong Moo

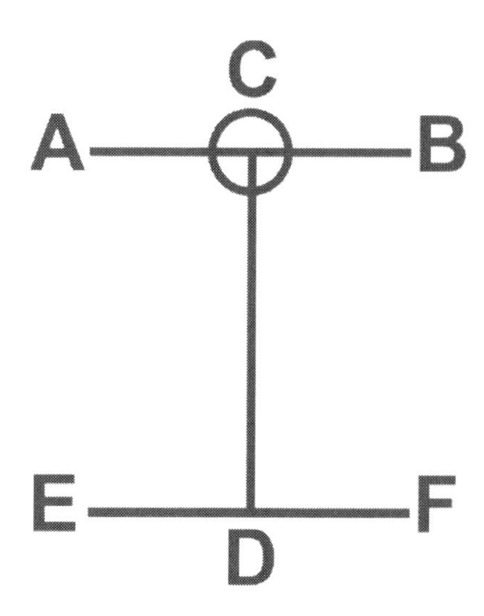


**The Choong Moo pattern refers to one of the greatest admirals of the Y Dynasty, Yi Soon-Sin. This man is said to have developed the very first armoured battleship in 1592 called the Kobukson. This vessel is considered an ancestor to the modern submarine. The pattern finishes with a left hand attack, meant to represent Yi Soon-Sin's death. The Black belt pattern is made up of 30 movements.**

*Start:* Begin in a parallel ready stance.

1. Bring your left foot towards B, creating a right side L-stance oriented in the direction of B. Pair this stance with a twin knife-hand block.

2. Step your right foot towards B, creating a right side walking stance oriented in the direction of B. Perform a right high section front knife-hand strike toward B. Shift your left-side back hand until it meets the front of your forehead.

3. Shift your right foot towards A, rotating to the right to create a left side L-Stance oriented in the direction of A. Perform a middle section guarding knife-hand block also towards A.

4. Bring your left foot towards A, creating a left side walking stance oriented in the direction of A. Initiate a left high section flat finger tip thrust towards A.

5. Step your left foot towards D, creating a right side L-stance oriented in the direction of D. Pair this stance with a middle position knife-hand guarding block also towards D.

6. Rotate until you are facing C, creating a left bending ready stance "A" oriented in the direction of C.

7. Perform a right middle section side piercing kick towards C.

8. Bring your right foot down towards C, creating a right side L-stance oriented in the direction of D. Pair this with a middle section knife-hand guarding block also towards D.

9. Initiate a right flying side piercing kick towards C. Shift your right foot towards D then bring it down also in the direction of D to create a left side walking stance oriented in the direction of D. Perform a middle section knife-hand guarding block also towards D.

10. Step your left foot towards E, rotating to the left to create a right side L-stance oriented in the direction of E. Pair this with a left low section forearm block also towards E.

11. Stretch your hand up as though you were about to grasp your opponent's head. Meanwhile assume a left side walking stance in the direction of E.

12. Perform a right high section knee kick towards E while bringing both hands down.

13. Bring your right foot down towards your left foot before shifting your left foot towards F, creating a left side walking stance oriented in the direction of F. Initiate a right high section reverse front knife-hand kick towards F while dropping your left-side back hand beneath the joint of your right elbow.

14. Initiate a right high section turning kick towards DF before lowering your right foot down to meet the left. Continue through movement 15 quickly.

15. Perform a left middle section back piercing kick towards F.

16. Bring your left foot down towards F, creating a left side L-Stance oriented in the direction of E. Pair this with a middle section forearm guarding block also towards E.

17. Initiate a left middle section turning kick towards DE.

18. Bring your left foot down towards your right foot before shifting your right foot towards C to create a right fixed stance oriented in the direction of C. Pair this stance with a U-shape block also in the direction of C.

19. Simultaneously jump and rotate to the left before coming down into the original location in a left side L-Stance oriented in the direction of C. Perform a middle section knife-hand guarding block towards C.

20 . Bring your left foot towards C, creating a left side walking stance oriented in the direction of C. Perform a right side Low section upset fingertip thrust towards C.

21. Initiate a right side back strike towards D paired with a left low section forearm block towards C, assuming a right side L-stance oriented in the direction of C while tugging your left foot.

22. Shift your right foot towards C, creating a right side walking stance oriented in the direction of C. Perform a right middle section straight fingertip thrust also towards C.

23. Bring your left foot towards B and rotate to the left, forming a left side walking stance oriented in the direction of B. Pair this stance with a left high section double forearm block also towards B.

24. Step your right foot towards B, creating a sitting stance oriented in the direction of C. Pair this stance with a right middle section forward forearm block towards C. Follow this with a right high section back side strike also towards B.

25. Perform a right middle section side piercing kick towards A while rotating to the left before lowering your foot towards A.

26. Initiate a left middle section side piercing kick towards A while rotating to the right.

27. Bring your left foot down towards A, before performing an X-knife-hand checking block towards B. Assume a left side L-Stance oriented in the direction of B with a pivot along your left foot.

28. Step your left foot towards B, creating a left side walking stance oriented in the direction of B. Perform a twin upward palm block also towards B.

29. Shift your left foot along the AB line before initiating a right forearm rising block in the direction of A while assuming a right side walking stance.

30. Continue the right side walking stance oriented in the direction of A and perform a left middle section punch also towards A.

* Finish the pattern by bringing your left foot backwards into the ready posture.

# Black Belt (First Dan) and Beyond…

**For many people the Black Belt is seen as the pinnacle of Martial Arts achievement and it is indeed something to be extremely proud of. You have worked for many hours, learned many new skills and developed a deep understanding of TaeKwonDo.**

While you work through the colored belts the focus is usually on the next grade until you reach black, but once you hit the heady heights of your 1st Dan things change a little and this can throw some practitioners.

At black belt the emphasis shifts from regular grading every few months to longer periods, sometimes several years between assessments. This discourages some students when they no longer get the consistent re-assurance of a new grade every quarter.

However the role of a Black Belt is different to that of a colored belt and this distinction is important to realize if you are to continue as a successful Martial Artist.

Gradings become fewer and further apart because the focus has now shifted from what you can do for yourself to what you can do for others. At 1st Dan other students now look up to you as a role model and in turn you are expected to become a teacher and mentor to those still on the colored belt journey.

This is not to say you shouldn't continue improving your skills and strive for 2[nd] Dan and beyond but instead of thinking *"what can I get from Taekwondo?"* now consider *"what can I give to others within Taekwondo"*.

As a coach and example to others you now shape the future of the style and the direction TaeKwonDo takes.

This selfless attitude is the difference between a good Black Belt and a great Black Belt.

# Thank you (and a Free Book!)

**It's important to realize that training in any Martial Art is a very personal experience and you will always get out what you put in. I hope you enjoy it!**

So thanks for reading this guide. I work hard to create useful and easy to follow guides for Martial Arts, Fitness and Self Defense.

**Given that you now have a better understanding of Taekwondo, please help other readers and give this book 5 stars and a few words if you found it useful!**

Good reviews make a world of difference to authors and other readers alike.

Finally, for a **COMPLETELY FREE** Training Guide check out my site at:

www.PhilPierceBooks.com

Thanks again.
- *Phil*

# Other Books by Phil Pierce

**Check out some of the other Martial Arts, Fitness and Well-Being titles from Phil Pierce:**

*How to Meditate in Just 2 Minutes: Easy Meditation for Beginners and Experts Alike*

**Given, Meditation can be an incredibly powerful tool in improving both physical and mental health, focus and relaxation but most people think it takes a long time to see results. The truth is it doesn't!**

With this easy-to-use book you can quickly learn how to achieve these incredible benefits in just 2 Minutes a day…

*How to Defend Yourself in 3 Seconds (or Less): The Self Defense Secrets You Need to Know!*

With most violent encounters the ability to defend yourself comes down to a matter of seconds where the right actions can be the difference between life and death.

Developed with input from Top Martial Artists and Self Defense experts this illustrated guide reveals the secrets of real Self Defence and exposes the truth behind street violence.

All designed to give you straight-forward, practical advice and keep you safe when it counts...

*How to Stretch for Martial Arts and Fitness: Your Ultimate Flexibility and Warm Up Guide!*

**Unlock the potential in your body with "How to Stretch for Martial Arts and Fitness: Your Ultimate Flexibility and Warm Up Guide!"**

A simple and insightful guide for beginners and experts alike - Grab Your Copy Now!

77130962R00057

Made in the USA
Columbia, SC
15 September 2017